Two-Up Motorcycle Riding

A Beginner's Guide for Riders and Passengers

Two-Up Motorcycle Riding

A Beginner's Guide for Riders and Passengers

Mario Orsini

Acknowledgements

It would be tough to write a book about two-up motorcycle riding without having a lot of experience riding two-up. While throughout my time riding, I've given rides to many people on the back of my bikes to include, friends, family and acquaintances, it's Kristen who has logged tens of thousands of miles (or kilometers) on the pillion so she deserves some major credit.

I also want to thank Alain Hoffman, Colin Phillips, and Tod Chapman for taking the time to not only proofread my book, but for also providing me excellent suggestions and feedback along the way. *Two-Up Motorcycle Riding: A Beginner's Guide for Riders and Passengers* is a much better book thanks to their contributions.

Table of Contents

Preface

I've been riding motorcycles since I was 5 years old and at the time of this being published I've been riding on the street for over 20 years. I was fortunate to grow up in a family of motorcyclists, and motorcycles have always been a part of my life.

After graduating college, I spent a couple of summers participating in amateur road racing in the Championship Cup Series on a Suzuki SV650S. Last year, I started racing again, but this time off road, participating in hare scrambles on my KTM 250 XC-F. I'm currently toying around with the idea of entering some mini-gp races or even some flat track racing.

As much as I enjoy the competition of racing, it's motorcycle travel I enjoy the most. There's nothing like packing up your bike and heading out on the road for extended periods of time. So far, I've ridden to and in all 49 of the Continental United States, and all but 3 of the states I've ridden two-up with my fiancé, Kristen on the back.

While my history with motorcycles goes back over 30 years, Kristen's just started after we met about 4 years ago. Since that time, she's acquired her motorcycle endorsement and has done some riding on both the street and in the dirt. She's also racked up tens-of-thousands of miles as a passenger on the back of my bikes.

I just wanted to give you a brief introduction to Kristen and our backgrounds in motorcycling since she is referenced throughout the book. If you're a loyal subscriber to my YouTube channel, **2 WHEELED RIDER**, you probably already knew all that stuff so turn the page to start learning something new!

Intro

Every month I read through dozens of motorcycle reviews from a handful of different motorcycle magazines to which I have subscriptions. Collectively they do a good job of giving me performance numbers, technical specifications, standard equipment and features, and optional accessories. They normally give a pretty good write up about their impressions of the bike to include handling, comfort, and the overall riding experience. Very seldom, if ever, do they mention what the bike is like with a passenger on the back, or what the ride is like from a passenger's point of view. Motorcycle passengers may be the most overlooked demographic in the motorcycle industry.

I can only speculate as to why motorcycle passengers are so often forgotten when it comes to motorcycle publications and marketing, but my guess is that is has to do with the fact that passengers don't buy motorcycles. While that may be true, we'd be wrong to assume they don't have an impact on bike purchases. When looking to buy my most recent touring bike, I took an extended test ride and then took Kristen on an extended test ride as well. I knew if she wasn't going to be comfortable riding on the back of the bike for hundreds of miles a day, there would be no reason for me to purchase it. According to the viewers of the motorcycle review videos on my YouTube

Channel, one of the most helpful parts of the review is when Kristen gives her impressions of the bike from the passenger's perspective.

Why I wrote this book

In doing research for this book, I found there to be very little information on the topic of riding with a passenger. Aside from a few short blog posts and the occasional mention in a motorcycle magazine there is almost nothing available on the topic. Most of the information that does exist is written for the rider with next to nothing written specifically for the passenger.

I wanted to write this book as a guide and manual for both the motorcyclist and the passenger. In my experience, most potential passengers fall into one of two categories; curious or scared. For potential passengers in the curious category, I believe they'll find a lot of valuable information in this book that will answer many of their questions. For those in the scared category, I think the information in this book will ease their mind a bit and hopefully encourage them to take a ride on a motorcycle.

Riding two-up is a lot of fun

Kristen and I take many multiple day motorcycle trips throughout the year. I can say it's a lot more fun traveling with her than it was when I traveled solo. Even if you don't have grand plans to travel all over the place and instead you just want someone to ride along with you to a local bike night or take a nice Sunday ride, I believe you'll find riding with a passenger can be a lot of fun and I hope you get a lot of value from this book.

Ride safe and have fun!

Chapter 1
Before You Begin

While this is the second shortest chapter, I would argue that it's also the most important one as skipping it could have serious legal or safety implications. Before putting anyone on the back of your motorcycle (or before you get on the back of anyone's motorcycle) there are three things you need to check.

Laws

Laws vary greatly from state to state and from country to country. I'm not a lawyer, nor am I an expert in every state's (or country's) traffic laws. I will not be giving you any specific guidance on local laws, except to say that **it is your responsibility to check local laws or the local laws of where you are planning to ride** before operating any motor vehicle on the road.

I bring up motorcycle laws in this book because some states have specific laws about who can have a passenger on the back of their motorcycle. For instance, as of this writing, in my home state of West Virginia, West Virginia Code 17B-2-5 states "No holder of a motorcycle instruction permit shall operate a motorcycle while carrying any passenger on the vehicle." So in my state while you can be issued a 90 permit to operate a motorcycle by successfully completing a written test, you must have also completed the riding test and have the full motorcycle endorsement in order to carry a passenger. Be sure to check with your local Department of Motor Vehicles or state website if you are unsure of the laws in your state.

If you are planning to ride abroad, you'll want to do some research while planning your trip. Be sure to check the local laws of all the places you're planning to ride as they could be very different from your home country.

Was your bike made to carry a passenger?

Believe it or not, not all motorcycles were designed to carry a passenger. While it should be common sense, check your bike's owner's manual to see if your bike can carry a passenger. If your bike doesn't have a rear seat or rear foot pegs or floorboards, then chances are it wasn't made to carry a passenger. DO NOT under any circumstances put someone on the back of your bike (or get on someone's bike) if it's not equipped to carry a passenger.

Check the weight limit

Every bike has a maximum amount of weight it can safely carry. While you can always find that information in your owner's manual, occasionally it will also be printed on a sticker on the bike. You may find it in one of two different forms; the gross vehicle weight rating (GVWR) or the carrying capacity. The GVWR is the total amount of weight including the weight of the bike, riders, luggage and anything else being hauled, the manufacturer has rated the bike to carry. If you subtract the wet weight of the bike (the bike with fuel, battery and other fluids) from the GVWR you'll have the weight you can safely add to the bike. Sometimes manufacturers will list the carry capacity. There's no math involved with the carry capacity as whatever number they have listed is the total amount of weight (riders, luggage, etc) that can be added to the bike.

Typically the GVWR and carry capacity totals from the manufacturers are a bit on the conservative side but I would still try to stay under their recommendation. Best case scenario if you go over the load capacity is the bike's handling will deteriorate under the added weight. The worst case scenario is something will fail on the bike because it's overloaded.

Also remember when calculating you and your passenger's weight to factor in your riding gear. Jackets, boots, and helmets can add quite a few pounds (kilograms) over your actual weight and need to be accounted in your total. When trying to figure out how much your passenger weighs you may want to tread lightly. While most men may not care, if you're planning to ask a lady her weight you may want to put your helmet on first, just in case she decides to rap you upside the head. That said a few moments of awkwardness for the sake of safety really shouldn't be an issue.

Finals Thoughts

If you're legally allowed to have a passenger, your bike was designed to carry a passenger, and your bike can handle the total weight of you and your passenger, you're ready to move onto the next chapter.

Chapter 2
The Rider

As a motorcycle rider, you have a big responsibility when carrying a passenger. Not only is their safety in your hands, but if they've never ridden a motorcycle before, then their first time out on your bike may shape future feelings about not only motorcycles but motorcyclists. Whether it's their first time on a bike or not, when a passenger is on your bike, it's NO time to show off. You should have three goals when it comes to carrying a passenger on your bike 1) make them feel safe 2) keep them safe and 3) make sure they have fun. Now I'm going to go over things you, as the rider, will need to be aware of when carrying a passenger.

Handling

Even the heaviest motorcycles weigh in at less than 1/3rd the weight of the average compact car with many weighing less than 1/6th. Adding 150 lb (68kgs) passenger to your 3,000lb (1,360kgs) car will only increase its overall weight by a mere 5%, so you're very unlikely to notice any difference in handling or performance. Put that same person on the back of your 500 lb

(227kgs) motorcycle and the total weight increases by 30%. Not only does the weight increase, but the center of gravity will also be higher. So what does more weight and a higher center of gravity mean? It means your handling is going to be negatively affected. We'll cover some things you can do to the bike in a later chapter to help the handling of your bike while carrying a passenger, but no matter how much tuning we do, your handling still won't be as stable as if you were riding solo.

The first thing you're going to notice when you go to lean your bike into a turn is that it's going to require more effort to steer when you have a passenger. Not only will the added weight require more effort to turn, but the bike will also turn in a bit slower because of the added mass. Also the added weight to the bike will cause the suspension to sag more, possibly leading to the suspension and ride feeling a bit "mushy." It's possible you could scrape your center stand, pegs or other hard parts in corners due to lower ground clearance as well. Some bikes will do a better job of handling passengers than others, but just be aware you're probably going to have to slow it down a bit in your favorite curves when you have someone riding on the back.

Braking

With a passenger you're going to need to allow more time and distance for stopping or slowing down. Due to the added weight, your brakes are now going to have to stop or slow more rolling mass with the same braking components and contact patch as when the bike only has the rider. You'll find you need additional distance and time to slow when you're riding on a downgrade. The steeper the grade, the longer it will take to slow or stop. The front brake or brakes provides 70-75% of the braking power with your rear brake providing the other 25-30%. You may find the rear brake provides more stopping power than usual when you're carrying a passenger because they are placing more weight over the rear wheel. I have found I use (and need) the rear brake more when Kristen is riding on the back than when I'm riding by myself. Also keep in mind; many newer bikes now come with linked brakes. Not all linked brakes work exactly the same but in their most basic form, engaging the front brake will also engage the rear brake and vice versa. Most modern motorcycles' braking systems are more than adequate to handle the added weight of a passenger, but just be aware you're not going to be able to stop as quickly.

Cornering Clearance

Cornering clearance will also be affected when riding with a passenger. The shock and forks will be further compressed than usual due to the added weight of the passenger. Because the suspension components are further compressed, the bike will have less ground clearance, meaning there will be less distance between the ground and the underside of the motorcycle. That will also mean your footpegs and center stand, if you have one, will be closer to the ground and more likely to drag when you lean into a corner. Since most footpegs have "feelers" they should keep you out of trouble should you start to drag hard parts. Those riding cruisers and similar style bikes, especially those with floorboards, will have to be more cognizant when cornering as those bikes already have very low ground clearance.

Passing

Adding a passenger to a motorcycle is going to significantly impact its power to weight ratio. Since the powertrain is being asked to move more weight down the road, it's not going to accelerate as fast as it does without a passenger. Remember to take the slower acceleration into account when planning to pass another vehicle. With the added weight, you'll need to allow more time and more distance to complete a pass. While perhaps not as important to consider on a four lane road, it's very important to take into account when passing another vehicle on a two lane road into oncoming traffic. If you have any hesitation or doubt, DO NOT even think about trying to make the pass.

Wind

Wind is one of those things that can be a minor annoyance all the way up to a serious danger when riding a motorcycle. In my own experience, I don't mind headwinds or tailwinds much. While a headwind can really cut down your fuel mileage, if you're riding behind a windshield, it shouldn't bother you much. Tailwinds aren't much of an issue either. Side winds however are a totally different story. While riding through the state of South Dakota, I had to lean my bike into the side wind in order to keep it upright. Riding a long distance with a strong side wind can really take its toll on you. Even worse than a strong side wind are strong side wind gusts. Side winds may cause you to have to lean into them in order to stay upright but a sustained wind is predictable. Side wind gusts are unpredictable, leading to dangerous riding conditions. A strong 30-40 mph (50-65 km/h) has enough power to knock you out of your lane if you're not expecting it.

As you may have guessed by now, side winds with a passenger on the back of your motorcycle will have more impact than when riding solo. The passenger makes up more surface area for the wind to hit further affecting your handling. There isn't much you can do to combat this other than to try to avoid hard side winds. It's also important to ask your passenger to remain as still as possible.

Smooth Inputs

Hard braking and sudden acceleration may be fine when you're riding solo but when you have a passenger in tow, you're going to need to smooth out your throttle, clutch and brake inputs. To get the bike moving it's going to require more finesse with the clutch lever and a little more throttle since the bike is carrying added weight. Passenger cars have seat belts to help keep you planted in the seat during braking and acceleration. A motorcycle rider can use the handlebars to brace himself under braking where the passenger is likely to slide forward under hard braking bumping into the rider. Similarly under hard acceleration the rider can hang onto the handlebars or clip-ons but will likely feel a tug from the passenger as they slide backward on the bike. The smoother the rider is with the inputs, the less the passenger will be moving around on the bike, making the ride better for both the rider and the passenger.

Final Thoughts

The six items above represent most of what you, as the rider, should expect while carrying a passenger. In Chapter 4 we'll go over a few things you can do to lessen the passenger's impact on the bike's ridability.

Chapter 3
The Passenger

As the passenger on the back of a motorcycle, you're putting your safety in the hands of another person. Please only get on the back of the bike of someone you trust and someone with whom you feel absolutely safe.

Safety First

Speaking of safety, we need to talk about proper riding gear. I'm going to discuss the **ABSOLUTE MINIMUM** in safety gear you should be wearing as a passenger. Since your brain is the most important part of your body we'll first go over a proper fitting helmet. Personally I only wear full face helmets as they provide the ultimate in protection fully covering your entire head and face. Most riders will have a spare or old helmet in the garage to loan you but it needs to fit properly otherwise it's not going to be able to provide much protection in the case of an accident. A helmet should fit your head snugly like a knit winter cap (beanie) but not so tight that it causes discomfort. Also look for a Department of Transportation (DOT) sticker on the helmet. Only those helmets (in the U.S.) with DOT stickers are legal for on road use. Economic Commission for Europe (ECE) approved helmets are required in a total of 47 countries including all of Europe. For all other parts of the world, please consult your local helmet laws. Be sure to check for any damage to the helmet to include deep scratches, dents, or cracks. If it looks less than perfect, I wouldn't trust it to protect my head.

The next thing you need are close toed shoes. Sandals, flip-flops and other open toed shoes (or no shoes at all) should NOT be worn. A good over the ankle, leather hiking boot makes a pretty good riding shoe but even a tennis shoe is better than sandals. Wear the heaviest duty footwear you have available.

You should always wear full length pants. A quality jean is about as good as you're going to get before buying motorcycle-specific riding apparel. In addition to protecting your skin in the event of an accident, long pants will also keep rocks and other debris from hitting your bare skin. I would also recommend a long sleeve t-shirt as well. I realize it won't protect as well as a riding jacket but as I stated at the beginning of this section, I'm only covering the absolute minimum. A long sleeve t-shirt will not only protect you skin from road debris but also from sun and windburn. Finally, if you have a pair of gloves, any pair of gloves, wear them.

Mounting and Dismounting

As silly as it may sound, you may need to practice getting on and off the bike a few times. You'll want to be especially careful when mounting or dismounting a bike with saddlebags to not kick the bag with your foot (motorcycle owners REALLY hate that). Be aware that motorcycles with saddlebags and/or trunks are a little trickier to get on and off of than your typical motorcycle.

Once you've determined you can successfully mount the bike, check to make sure none of your clothing is near any moving parts like the wheels or chain of the bike. Also ensure your feet can reach the foot pegs or floorboards of the motorcycle. Your feet need to remain on the pegs at all times.

Staying on the Bike

Unlike automobiles, motorcycles don't have seat belts to keep you in place on the machine. Instead you're going to have to hold on yourself. How you securely stay on the motorcycle is going to vary from bike to bike but there are basically three main methods.

Hanging On

In most cases you're probably going to hold onto the rider.

You'll want to hold the rider by gripping him/her on the sides of his/her waist or find something else on them to hang onto such as his/her belt. One thing you don't want to do is "hug" the rider. Hugging the rider (wrapping your arms all the way around him/her) will not only make it uncomfortable for the rider but also will take away your ability to brace yourself under braking.

Using the Grab Rails

Some motorcycles are equipped with grab rails. Instead of holding directly to the rider, the passenger can hang onto the bike by utilizing the grab rails. Grab rails aren't usually found on sport bikes but can be regularly found on more touring-oriented bikes. As long as the rider isn't accelerating or decelerating too quickly, grab rails are an effective way to stay on the back of a motorcycle.

Just Hanging Out

Believe it or not, there are some motorcycles that the passenger doesn't need to hold onto the rider or the bike. They are built in such a way that it would be nearly impossible for the passenger to fall off the back of the bike. I remember riding on the back of my uncle's old Honda Gold Wing GL1200 when I was a kid and falling asleep on it. I'm pretty certain Kristen has fallen asleep on the back of my Yamaha FJR1300 as well (though I know she won't admit it). Since both of the bikes I mentioned are equipped with top cases or "trunks," it's impossible for a passenger to slide off the back of the motorcycle. Just because it's easier to stay on the bike doesn't mean you should go to sleep. You still need to pay attention to what's going on around you.

With all of the above methods, keep your feet on the foot pegs AT ALL TIMES!

Cornering

Since motorcycles only have two wheels they do not corner or turn the same way as a car. Cars are steered into turns with all four tires remaining on the road at all times. Motorcycles are counter-steered into turns. When going through a right hand corner, the rider actually points the front wheel to the left causing the bike to turn to the right. Another thing that's different about motorcycles are their tires. A car tire is always perpendicular to the ground; the tread area of a car tire is also very flat. A motorcycle tire however can have a very convex shape. The convex shape of the motorcycle tire allows the rider to change the angle of the bike while cornering and still maintain the tire's contact patch. Some of the world's top riders can reach lean angles of greater than 60 degrees!

When I'm giving the passenger a briefing (I'll go into detail about a briefing in a later chapter) about what to do in turns, some may think they will need to lean in the opposite direction of me and the bike to keep the bike from "falling over." Nothing could be further from the truth! I normally tell my passengers to not do anything or just stay behind me. By not doing anything the passenger will naturally lean with the rider and the bike. Saying "Just stay behind me" accomplishes the same exact thing. Once a passenger becomes a little more proficient and comfortable riding on a motorcycle he/she will be able to better anticipate the upcoming curve or turn and begin to look over the rider's inside shoulder. But for now, just hang on and have fun.

Sit Still

Most motorcycles are made up of two front forks and either one or two rear shocks. They are also being balanced by the rider at all times whether it be moving forward in an upright position, leaning over in a corner, or stopping at a light with the rider's feet down. Because motorcycles are very light (compared to cars), it's very easy to upset their suspension. For that reason, you'll want to sit still on the back of the bike. Do NOT make any sudden or jerky movements while riding on the bike. It could result in loss of control of the bike for the rider which means you could both be injured. Be sure to keep both feet on the pegs at all times, do not attempt to stand up, keep your hands and arms tucked in at all times and keep facing forward.

No Head-butting

If you want to get an invite to go riding again, do NOT head-butt the rider. I don't think any of my passengers have intentionally head-butted me on a ride but intentional or not, I'm not happy when my expensive helmet gets scratched. The best way to keep from head-butting the rider is to pay attention. Anticipate stopping at the red light ahead or slowing for the approaching corner, know the brakes are about to be applied and brace yourself accordingly.

Final Thoughts

As you can see, being the passenger on a motorcycle makes you an active participant in the ride. If you follow the advice discussed in this chapter, you should have a safe and fun ride.

Chapter 4
The Bike

In this chapter we're going to go over some things you can do to your bike to make it more suitable for carrying a passenger, as well as discuss different types of motorcycles and what to expect from them in regards to carrying passengers. These are all general recommendations. You should also check your owner's manual for specific information about your specific make and model.

Suspension Set Up

On most motorcycles when we talk about suspension, we are talking about the front forks and a rear shock(s). There are some notable exceptions such as the latest Honda Gold Wing which now features a double wishbone front suspension or the BMW GS bikes which uses a telelever suspension up front. There have also been some other exceptions over the years. Since the overwhelming majority of bikes on the road use the traditional suspension set up of forks up front and a shock(s) in the rear, that's what we are going to cover in this book. However, much of the information is still applicable regardless of suspension type.

Adjustable vs. Non-adjustable Suspension

Unfortunately, not all motorcycles come with adjustable suspensions. Suspension components can be very expensive. By using "budget" suspension components, the manufacturers are able to keep the costs down when producing bikes. Your bike's suspension settings can still be changed by using different weight oil, changing springs, changing valves, or a handful of other things that are too complex to go into detail about in this book.

Adjustable Suspension

A fully adjustable suspension will allow you to adjust the preload, compression and rebound. Not all bikes with adjustable suspensions will have fully adjustable components front and rear. It's not unheard of to have a fully adjustable front fork and a rear shock with only preload adjustment. Next we'll cover what preload, compression and rebound actually do.

Preload

The preload adjuster bears down on the fork or shock spring to either shorten or extend it. Preload is used to adjust the fork or shock to the correct range of operation within the suspension travel. More preload will raise the bike up keeping it near the top of its travel while less preload will have the bike sitting lower and closer to the bottom of its suspension travel.

Compression Damping

Compression damping is what gives the bike a soft or stiff feel. The compression damping determines how fast the suspension compresses when you hit a bump or imperfection. With compression damping too stiff, the fork or shock can't compress quickly enough when hitting a bump. This causes the wheel to rise up the face of the bump, transferring it into the chassis of the bike where you'll feel it. If your compression damping is too soft, it will give the bike a "floating" feeling.

Rebound Damping

Your suspension compresses when going over a bump, rebound damping determines how fast the suspension can extend to keep the tire in contact with the ground. With too much rebound damping, the suspension will stay compressed when it should be extending to the road on the downside of the bump, causing the tire to lose contact with the ground. Conversely, with too little rebound, the suspension will extend too quickly, forcefully pushing the bike up and giving it a loose feeling.

Setting Your Suspension

The best place to start is your owner's manual. If your bike has an adjustable suspension and a rear pillion then there is a good chance your owner's manual will give you some suggested settings which should provide you with a good baseline. In many cases, you'll adjust the preload to compensate for the extra weight the bike's suspension will have to handle due to the added passenger. Please keep in mind these are only suggestions. There's a big difference between adding a 100 lb (45 kg) person to the back of your bike or a person who weighs 200 lbs (90 kg) so you may have to further tune your settings. If you don't know much about suspension set up, just use what your manual recommends; it'll be better than leaving it alone.

Electronic Suspension

Some higher-end bikes now come with electronically-adjustable suspensions allowing you to adjust the suspension just by pressing a few buttons. The KTM I currently ride has suspension modes preset for the following: Rider, Rider + Luggage, Rider + Passenger, Rider + Passenger + Luggage. I've ridden bikes from Yamaha and Ducati with similar setups. These electronic suspensions make it super-convenient to adjust your suspension settings and remove a lot of the guesswork. If you find the factory presets aren't working as well as you'd like in most cases your dealer can make some changes electronically to tune it more to your liking.

Tires

I check my tires before every ride. I begin with a visual check for punctures or other damage, and then I check the tire pressure using a gauge. While I do have a Tire Pressure Monitoring System (TPMS) on my bike, I use it as a supplement to a gauge. It's important to make sure your tires are in good shape before taking any ride but especially important to check them before riding two-up. They will be placed under more load than usual due to the added weight of the passenger. It's a good idea to check your owner's manual to see if it recommends changing the tire pressure for two-up riding. In some cases, the manufacturer will recommend adding a few more psi (or bar) to compensate for the added weight.

Types of Motorcycles

There are many different models and types of motorcycles available on the market today. I've broken them down into five basic groups to speak in some general terms about what you can expect from each type of motorcycle when it comes to hauling a passenger.

Standard Motorcycle

Many standard motorcycles such as the Suzuki SV650 or the Yamaha FZ-07 come with a bare bones suspension with little to no adjustability. In the Yamaha's case the only adjustability is rear preload. The good thing about a standard motorcycle is they are normally equipped with an adequate rear seat and will usually have the passenger sitting in a fairly upright position.

Cruiser

Cruisers, especially the sportier ones, will sometimes have adjustable suspensions. If the suspension is adjustable, be sure to follow the manual's settings for two-up riding. Due to the limited suspension travel of cruisers, it would be very easy to bottom out the suspension if improperly set up. When it comes to rear seats on cruisers, it's hit or miss. The passenger could be sitting on a wide, plush, leather seat or one that feels like a block of wood. Usually, the passenger will have an upright if not slightly leaned back seating position. With cruisers sitting so low to the ground, don't expect much in the way of legroom as it can get rather cramped for a passenger.

Sport Bike

Quality sport bikes almost always have fully adjustable suspensions and while that may be good news for the rider, there isn't much good news for the passenger. On the back of a sport bike a passenger can expect to be cramped, leaned forward and sitting on a brick for a seat. While most sport bikes can technically carry a passenger, they weren't designed with passenger comfort in mind. These bikes are derived from race bikes. They're meant to go fast, stop quickly, and handle well. Riding on the back of a sport bike can be a lot of fun if you keep the rides short.

Dual Sport

Much like sport bikes, the passenger on a dual sport bike is an afterthought. Heck, some dual sport bikes aren't set up to carry a passenger at all! With there being many levels of dual sports from your cheaper Japanese air-cooled bikes, like the Kawasaki KLX250 to your more expensive European liquid-cooled bikes, such as the KTM 690 Enduro R, suspensions can range from no adjustments to fully adjustable suspensions. If the bike is set up to carry a passenger, expect one of the most uncomfortable seats ever. Most feel like a 2x6 with a piece of vinyl stapled to it.

Touring Bike

While there are some major differences between sport tourers like the Yamaha FJR1300, adventure tourers like the BMW GS bikes and tourers such as the Gold Wing, I've decided to lump them all into the Touring Bike category because they are the best in passenger comfort. Nearly all touring bikes come with fully adjustable suspensions with many of them being electronically adjustable. The passenger will have an upright seating position and in most cases a comfortable seat to sit on. On some of the larger tourers, they may also have a backrest. The touring bikes will also offer the passenger the most amount of legroom of any type of motorcycle. If there is a negative, it's for the rider in this case and not the passenger. Touring bikes are normally some of the heaviest bikes made which can make them tougher to maneuver especially at low speeds. Adding another 100-200+ lbs (45-90+ kgs) won't make the bike any easier to handle.

Final Thoughts

It's important to check your owner's manual for suspension and tire recommendations before placing a passenger on the back of your motorcycle. Taking a few extra minutes to make some minor adjustments can have a huge impact on the quality and safety of your ride.

Chapter 5
Getting Started

As with most things, it's best to start slow and build. In this chapter, we'll discuss how to introduce someone to the world of motorcycle riding.

Short Rides

It's best to begin with shorter rides. The first time someone takes a motorcycle ride, there's a good chance they'll be on sensory-overload. Keep the rides short to start so you can talk to your passenger and find out how they are doing. Ask them what they enjoyed and what they didn't like about the ride. If someone is brand new to riding, I will even check on them at the first stop sign/stop light to ensure they're doing ok. As we discussed earlier, some bikes are not very comfortable for passengers, so a shorter ride can make for a much greater experience for the passenger than a longer ride. On the flip side, if they are riding on the back of a really comfortable bike, they may fall asleep. Suddenly awakening on the back of a motorcycle for the first time could make for quite a startle and the last thing I want as a rider is someone making sudden movements on the back of my bike. Also, in many cases new passengers are not going to have the best riding gear, so shorter rides will keep them safer and more comfortable on the back of the bike.

As your passenger gets more comfortable riding, feel free to start making the rides longer. However, don't neglect to work in some stop time allowing them to stretch and be off the bike for a while. Their endurance as a passenger will grow just like your endurance as a rider. It's not going to happen overnight but the more they ride with you, the more comfortable they'll become and the more miles (kilometers) they'll be able to cover.

Briefing

It's imperative to give your passenger a briefing to ensure both your safety and theirs before their first ride. In addition to providing them much needed guidance on what to do and what to expect on the bike, it will also make them feel much safer and more at ease. There are many things you can brief them on including things discussed earlier in the book. I would recommend to first start with a brief explanation of the route you have planned including how long you plan to ride and where you'll be stopping (if you plan on stopping at all). I would also cover such things as how to mount and dismount the motorcycle, why they need to wear a helmet, how to hang on, what they need to do in a corner, and the importance of not making sudden movements. You may also want to go over some signals should they need your attention (I'll discuss this later in the chapter). These are my recommendations, but you may have some other things you feel are important to share with your passenger before the ride. My only other recommendation would be to keep it brief (hence calling it a briefing). Giving them too much instruction could cause confusion. It's best to go over the most important stuff and then later build on what they've learned.

Communication

High end touring bikes have had helmet communications for a very long time. However, it wasn't until the last few years that helmet communications have become more mainstream on other types of motorcycles thanks to smartphones and bluetooth technology. The ability to communicate with your passenger via a helmet headset is invaluable. It will enable you to get real time feedback from them to ensure they are doing well and let them know what's coming up ahead. Additionally, they'll feel safer because it's super easy for them to ask you to slow down if the ride is starting to make them uncomfortable or just be more comfortable knowing they can give you instant feedback.

What if you don't have communication systems in yours and your passenger's helmets? No need to worry; that's the way it used to be up until a few years ago and we still managed to survive. You just need to come up with a few basic signals. Signals for "pull over," "slow down," and "I'm ok" should cover it.

Longer Rides

Once your riding companion becomes more comfortable on the bike you can start lengthening the rides. The distance they'll be able to travel or even want to travel will vary greatly depending on the bike and the individual. Just be sure to plan to stop for quick breaks every hour or so. Over time they may be able to "ride out the tank," meaning ride until the bike runs out of fuel. Riding out the tank obviously varies depending on the type of bike. For instance, my FJR1300 could go 200-240 miles (320-390 kms) on a tank while my DRZ-400SM could only go about 90 miles (144 kms) until I added a higher capacity fuel tank. The point is: if your passenger is having fun riding, feel free to start going on longer rides but build up to it so you can ensure they're still having fun.

Gear

If you're riding two-up more often and especially for longer distances, it's time to get serious about safety and make sure your passenger is properly outfitted. As I mentioned earlier, not only will proper riding gear keep your passenger safer, it will also keep them more comfortable as riding gear is specifically made to wear on the bike.

It's important to let your passenger pick out their own gear but that doesn't mean you can't help. Take them to your local dealer or motorcycle apparel store so they can try some stuff on to see how it fits. When it comes to gear, generally you get what you pay for. Make sure the helmet has minimum of a DOT approval (for the U.S.) but a SNELL or ECE rating is preferred. For jackets, pants and boots, a CE rating is a plus.

Headset

While there's nothing wrong with hand signals, headset technology has come a long way in the last few years and bluetooth headsets have become very affordable. A good headset can aid in making sure your passenger has a safer and more enjoyable time on the bike. Being able to communicate in real time will allow the passenger to give the rider instant feedback if there is a problem or to just let them know they're doing fine. It will also give the rider the ability to give the passenger instructions or warnings. Additionally, once your passenger becomes more seasoned at riding on the back of the bike they may just want to chill out and listen to some music. A bluetooth headset will allow them to stream their favorite tunes or possibly listen to an audiobook while enjoying the ride.

Aerodynamics

Most things on a motorcycle are designed with the rider in mind and not a lot of thought given to the passenger; aerodynamics are no exception. On many motorcycles, the passenger seat sits a few inches (centimeters) above the rider seat so the passenger's helmet may be above the rider's. On my FJR1300, I couldn't run the touring windscreen at max height (it had an electronically-adjustable windscreen) without it causing a lot of wind buffeting for Kristen. I bring this up because you should check with your passenger to see how they are doing with the wind. In the case of sport bikes and naked bikes, there likely isn't much you can do, but with touring bikes and some cruisers you may have some adjustability of the windscreen or even the ability to swap screens to make the ride more enjoyable for your passenger.

Final Thoughts

When it comes to riding with a passenger you need to start with short rides and slowly build up to longer ones. But the most important thing is to ensure your passenger is safe AND having a great time!

Chapter 6
Traveling with a Passenger

It's no secret that I love to tour on my motorcycle. Fortunately, I've been lucky enough to find someone that enjoys traveling with me on the back of the bike. If you're fortunate to find someone who's willing to ride longer distances on multiple days on the back of your bike, congratulations! In this chapter, I'll share with you some tips to help you keep your passenger happy.

Trip Planning

If you're going to be traveling with a passenger, you need to allow them to have some input on the planning. On our trips, I normally take care of planning the general route and major highlights of the trip and then Kristen likes to find cool restaurants and lesser known things to check out along the way. It may work differently with your passenger and some may be fine with letting you plan the whole trip, but I would still offer them the opportunity to help.

Mileage (Distance)

You're going to need to take your passenger into account when planning your travel route. While you may be able to handle 400 mile (643 kilometer) days, they may only be able to handle 300 miles (482 kilometers) per day, or even less. It will be hard to determine how far they can ride comfortably on back-to-back, or even back-to-back-to-back days so error on the side of less miles (kilometers) rather than too many. Once they become more seasoned, it will be much easier to gauge.

You're also going to need to take your own endurance into account. Riding long distances solo is one thing but riding long distance with a passenger is much more demanding on the rider. If you're riding mostly straight highways and interstates, it likely won't be too bad unless you start experiencing a lot of side winds. However, if you're riding roads with a lot of twists and turns, the added weight of the passenger is going to start to wear you down over the course of the ride. Again, it will take some time and experience to figure out what works best for you and your passenger.

Luggage

On my current touring bike the saddlebag on the left side is larger than the one on the right. I'm sure you can guess which one I get stuck using. Kristen always gets the larger of the two bags. It's important to make sure to allow your passenger plenty of storage space on the bike when traveling. If your bike is equipped with hard bags, I would suggest investing in a set of bag liners to help ensure your passenger doesn't over pack. If their items fit in the bag liner then they'll also fit in the saddlebag. It also makes unloading at the end of the day much easier as the bag liners are very convenient to carry into the hotel room for the night.

If you decide to use saddlebags on your motorcycle, always be sure to distribute the weight evenly on each side so you don't negatively affect the handling characteristics of the bike.

Additional Comforts

Comfortable riding gear for distance riding is a must. I would also recommend a good rain suit or waterproof riding gear because mother nature is tough to predict, especially on longer trips. While I've yet to buy any for myself, heated gear is also a favorite of many tourers and commuters. Heated gear prices have fallen in recent years making it more affordable to own. Heated gear can be wired to the bike, battery powered or a combination of the two. It can definitely help make a chilly morning ride much more comfortable.

There are all sorts of aftermarket items to help make

passenger more comfortable, and a comfortable passenger also means a more enjoyable ride for the both of you. Not sure what will make your passenger more comfortable? Ask them what hurts at the end of a long ride? If it's their knees, maybe some footpeg extenders would help. Butt? Try a seat cover/cushion or a new seat. Back? See if a backrest/sissy bar or even a top case with an integrated backrest is available. Shoulders? Maybe a set of armrests would help. Neck? A lighter or more aerodynamic helmet.

Finals Thoughts

These are just a few tips to get you started traveling on a motorcycle with a passenger. If you'd like more information on motorcycle travel, please check out my book *Motorcyclist's Guide To Travel.*

Chapter 7
Your Next Bike

It's been said that the perfect number of motorcycles to own is N +1. If you are now riding two-up more often, you may have some additional things to consider when purchasing your next motorcycle.

Passenger Input

If you're planning to use your bike for two-up riding, I would suggest allowing your passenger some input on your next motorcycle purchase. Take them with you when you head to the dealer so they can see the bike for themselves and even sit on the pillion (be sure to ask first) to see how it feels. Another good option is to attend a motorcycle show. Most manufacturers attend the larger shows and encourage you to throw a leg over the bike to see how it feels.

Test Ride

If you've been around motorcycles long, you know finding a dealer that allows test rides is like finding a unicorn, but I can promise you they do exist. I'm fortunate to have two different dealerships close by that not only allow demo rides but have demo bikes specifically for that purpose. You may have to do some searching or asking around but before buying your next bike you should really take it out for a test ride. Be sure to take your passenger along as well so they can also get a feel for the bike on the test ride. Before buying my KTM 1290 Super Adventure, Kristen and I took it on an all-day ride to see how it would do. If she hadn't been comfortable on the back, there would have been no sense in me buying it.

If you're unable to find a dealer that will allow test rides, all hope is not lost. You can attend a "demo event". Most manufacturers host demo events throughout the year. Larger motorcycle events such as Daytona Bike Week or even some racing events will have multiple manufacturers present with demo bikes for you to test ride. Some manufacturers will show up with a trailer load of demo bikes and host a demo day at your local dealership. Most major manufacturers have a demo day page on their website with dates, times and other information. With a little online searching, I'm sure you'll be able to find a place or event that will allow you to take a test ride.

Reviews

Finding motorcycle reviews that cover the comfort of the passenger are more difficult to find than dealerships who allow test rides. Some magazines will discuss passenger comfort and amenities on the luxury touring bikes like the Honda Gold Wing or BMW K 1600 GTL, but seldom mention the passenger on your sportier or standard models. On the 2 Wheeled Rider YouTube Channel, I try to get Kristen on the back of every bike I review so the viewers can get her perspective when it comes to comfort, ride, etc. and my point of view when it comes to handling, braking and several other things with a passenger on the back.

Final Thoughts

If you plan to spend a lot of time two-up riding, allow your passenger some input on your next bike purchase to make sure they stay comfortable and happy. While I like taking some solo rides from time to time, it's much more fun traveling with Kristen on the back of the bike than going at it alone.

Chapter 8
What's Next?

If someone is a frequent passenger on the back of a motorcycle, then to me they are part of the motorcycle community. In this final chapter, I want to point out how passengers can get more involved in the motorcycle community.

Passenger Only

Let's face it. Not everyone wants to pilot a motorcycle; some are just content to ride on the back and that's ok. There are some other aspects of the sport they may want to get involved in or find interests them.

Trip Planning

As I discussed earlier in the book, Kristen and I share the travel planning duties of our motorcycle trips. You may find your passenger enjoys finding cool places to travel to and things to do along the way. If that's what they like doing, great!

Rallies and Show

Try taking your passenger to some local motorcycle rallies or shows. Some of the larger rallies and shows will have all sorts of motorcycles and motorcycle-related products on display. There's also usually some great food, beer and lots of activities going on throughout the events. Rallies and shows are just another way you can further expose them to the motorcycle community while also having a lot of fun.

Races

While in this book, we're talking specifically about motorcycle passengers, I would highly suggest taking any of your non-motorcycle riding friends or family to a motorcycle race. I haven't taken anyone yet that didn't have an outstanding time. Kristen has become a race fan over the last few years. I'm pretty certain she can name the entire starting grid for MotoGP and most of the AMA Supercross 250 and 450 main event riders. I'd argue I'm still the bigger race fan of the two of us but then I'm reminded of the time she got Valentino Rossi to sign her pit pass and kept rubbing it in my face. Together we've attended multiple MotoGP, Moto2, Moto3 and MotoAmerica races. We've also been to Supercross which I would say is one of the most fan and family friendly sporting events you can attend. On a more local and regional level, we've attended club road racing, hare scrambles and enduros. I've also attended motocross and hill climb events. You can really learn a lot about motorcycles at these types of events and have fun doing it.

Future Rider

Some passengers won't be content staying on the back of the bike and will soon want to move up to the front seat to have even more fun. The best way to learn to ride a motorcycle is to get some training. There are many different training classes available. I suggest doing an online search to see what's available in your area. In this section, I'll touch on just a few of the training courses including some I've personally attended.

MSF Basic RiderCourse

I've never actually taken the Motorcycle Safety Foundation (MSF) Basic RiderCourse but have friends and family who have. I've also watched a few sessions of the training. The MSF class is a good place to start for those who have no idea how to ride a motorcycle. Prices will vary depending on location but this course is one of the cheaper ones and also provides you with a motorcycle and helmet. Consisting of both classroom instruction and riding instruction the class can normally be completed over the course of a weekend. Most classes are held in large parking lots or some sort of closed course. In most states, the successful completion of this course will waive the license test meaning you can take your completion certificate to the DMV to receive your motorcycle endorsement. Many insurance companies also offer a motorcycle insurance discount to those who have successfully completed the course.

California Superbike School

Keith Code has been providing one-on-one motorcycle training since 1976 and has trained many championship winning riders, including World Superbike and Grand Prix champions. Despite the name, you don't have to go to California to go to the school. California Superbike School comes to many different tracks throughout the United States so chances are you'll find one near you. They offer single day and multiple day courses as well as courses specific to racing. They offer different levels of training as well; each one building on the previous class.

At Superbike school you train on sport bikes. When I last took the class we were on Kawasaki ZX6-R 636 models but currently they are using the BMW S1000RR as their school bikes. You are also able to use your own bike for some of the courses, assuming it meets the technical requirements. The typical schedule for the day is 20-30 minutes of in classroom instruction followed by 20-30 minutes on the track working on a specific drill or technique. You'll do that 5 times throughout the day so by the end of the day you'll have had about 2 hours of track time.

Superbike school isn't just meant for racers. While I was racing at the time I took the class, everything I learned that day was directly applicable to street riding as well. I had plenty of "a-ha" moments throughout the day and really felt like I learned more in one day about riding than I had in the previous 10 years combined. I can't recommend Keith Code's California Superbike School enough!

Cornerspin

If you don't feel comfortable riding a 400 lb (181 kgs), 200hp superbike, then maybe a 170 lb (77 kgs), 7hp dirt bike will be more your style. Chief Instructor Aaron Stevenson is the creator of Cornerspin: "Roadracing in the Dirt." The school, located in Salisbury, NC (about 45 minutes from the Charlotte Douglas International Airport), teaches you how to be a better street rider by placing you on small displacement dirt bikes, such as Honda CRF100s and Yamaha TTR125s, equipped with street tires, on a dirt track. Yes, you read that correctly! You're going to work on your street and track riding skills by training on a dirt bike on a dirt track. Make no mistake; this is NOT a dirt bike school.

There's a reason Marc Marquez, Valentino Rossi and many other top racers practice in the dirt. Training in the dirt allows you to work on throttle control, braking, riding with limited traction, controlling the slide, body positioning and many other aspects of riding that translate directly to the street or road racing. Riding small displacement dirt bikes allows you to push to the limit with limited risk of injury. The dirt track features hairpins, camber changes, elevation changes, fast transitions, decreasing and expanding radius turns, literally every type of situation you're going to face on the street or a race track.

Aaron spends 20-30 minutes teaching you a new technique and then you'll spend at least that long out on the track working on it. I was able to correct some of my own bad habits, which immediately improved my riding. Cornerspin is also one of the most affordable training schools to attend. I can't say enough good things about the two-day course which is why I'm planning to go back for a second time.

Final Thoughts

Whether your passenger decides to stay a passenger or decides to try out riding for themselves, I wish them the best on their journey. I hope you have found value in this book and I hope to see you out on the road one day!

Riding Schools

Motorcycle Safety Foundation

Various Locations

www.msf-usa.org

800-446-9227

msf@msf-usa.org

California SuperBike School

Various Locations

superbikeschool.com

800-530-3350

CornerSpin

Salisbury, North Carolina

www.cornerspin.com

704-332-3147

admin@cornerspin.com

Author Contact

Have a question or comment? Please don't hesitate to contact me. I'd love to hear from you!

Mario Orsini
PO Box 64
Bunker Hill, WV 25413

2wheeledriderdotcom@gmail.com

Website: 2wheeledrider.com

YouTube: **2 WHEELED RIDER**